STORMING PARADISE

Writer: Chuck Dixon
Artists: Butch Guice, Rick Burchett, Eduardo Barreto and Fernando Blanco

Colors: Carrie Strachan and Darlene Royer
Letters: Patrick Brosseau, Sal Cipriano

Covers by Butch Guice

Jim Lee	Editorial Director
Hank Kanalz	VP – General Manager
Ben Abernathy	Editor – Original Series
Kristy Quinn	Editor
Ed Roeder	Art Director

DC COMICS	
Paul Levitz	President & Publisher
Richard Bruning	SVP – Creative Director
Patrick Caldon	EVP – Finance & Operations
Amy Genkins	SVP – Business & Legal Affairs
Gregory Noveck	SVP – Creative Affairs
Steve Rotterdam	SVP – Sales & Marketing
Cheryl Rubin	SVP – Brand Management

SUSTAINABLE FORESTRY INITIATIVE Certified Fiber Sourcing www.sfiprogram.org
PWC-SFICOC-260

DC Comics, a Warner Bros. Entertainment Company.

ISBN: 978-1-4012-2545-2

HEY TOJO...

You're Next!

BUY WAR BONDS and STAMPS

...NOW, I AM BECOME SHIVA THE DESTROYER OF WORLDS...

...NOW, I AM BECOME DEATH THE DESTROYER OF WORLDS...
LOOK AT OPPENHEIMER.

...DESTROYER OF WORLDS...
HE'S TALKING TO HIMSELF.
NO, GENERAL GROVES...

HE IS ASSURING HIS PLACE IN HISTORY.

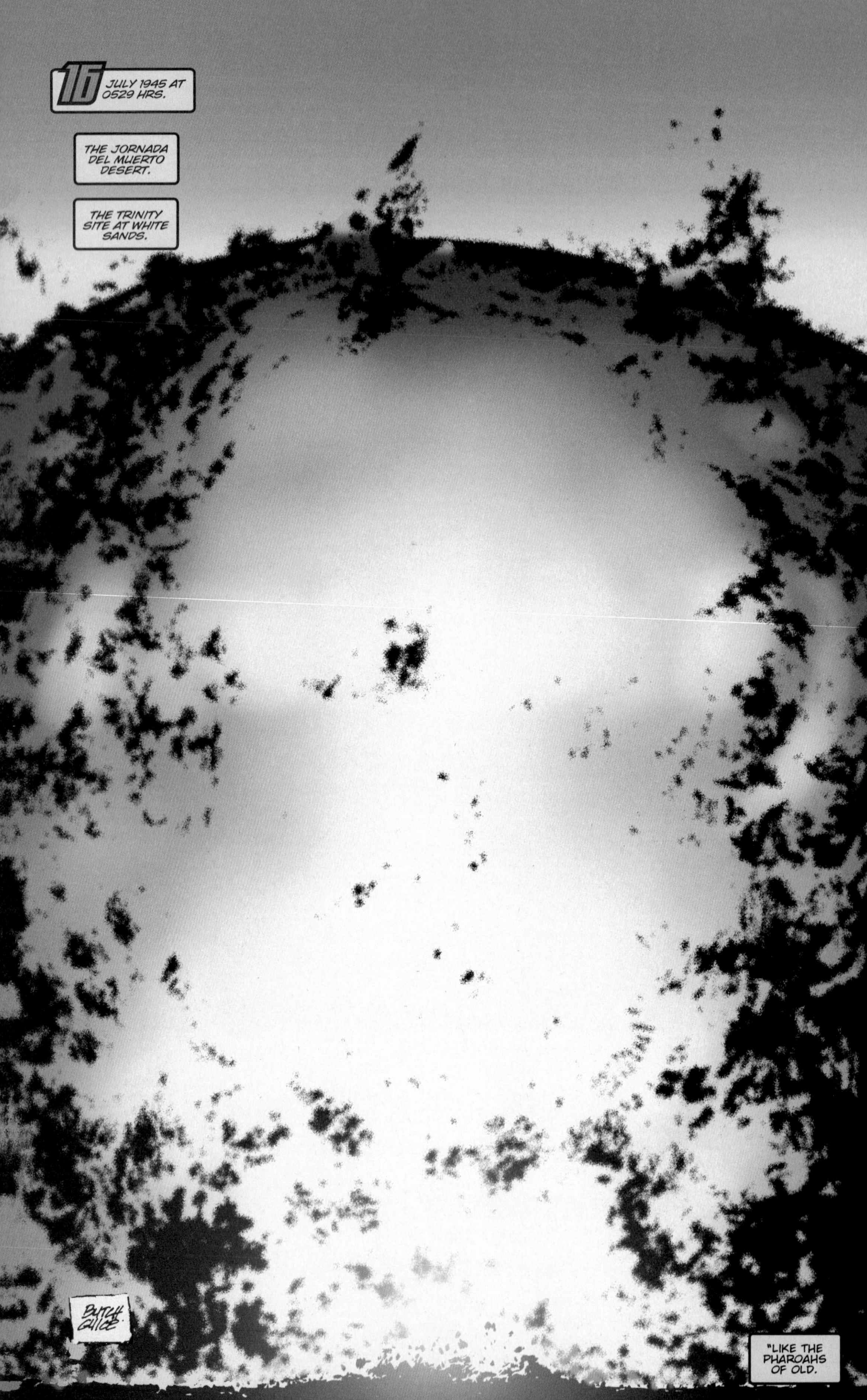
16 JULY 1945 AT 0529 HRS.
THE JORNADA DEL MUERTO DESERT.
THE TRINITY SITE AT WHITE SANDS.
BUTCH GUICE
"LIKE THE PHAROAHS OF OLD.

THE BUILDERS OF THE PYRAMIDS WOULD BE KILLED AND BURIED WITH THEIR SECRETS.
BABELSBERG, GERMANY
SITE OF THE TRIPARTITE CONFERENCE.

BAD NEWS, MISTER PRESIDENT?
THOSE EGGHEADS IN NEW MEXICO GOT A DECIMAL POINT IN THE WRONG PLACE.
OUR SECRET WEAPON BLEW UP IN THEIR FACES.

GROVES DEAD. FERMI DEAD. OPPENHEIMER DEAD.
THEY CAN'T EVEN GIVE ME AN ESTIMATE ON WHEN THEY'LL START UP AGAIN.

DO WE WAIT?
WE CAN'T, HANK.
WE CAN'T ALLOW THE JAPS A SECOND WIND.

INITIATE OLYMPIC.

21 JULY.
KUMOMOTO PREFECTURE, ISLAND OF KYUSHU.
THERE IS HONOR IN FIGHTING TO DEFEAT.
BUT NOT HERE, TAITO.

WE ARE BEING CRUSHED BY IRON AND NOT BY MEN.
THERE IS NO HONOR IN DEATH DELIVERED BY MACHINES.

I PREFER NOT TO SEE THE END.
I HAVE DONE MY PART IN BRINGING THIS ON. MY FAILURES HAVE DOOMED JAPAN.

WHAT OF ME, GENERAL-SAN?
WHAT ARE YOUR FINAL ORDERS?

DO NOT FOLLOW ME, TAITO.
YOU WILL REMAIN TO FACE WHAT COMES.

PLEASE, GENERAL-SAN!
I ASK THIS ONE LAST FAVOR!

I HAVE GIVEN MY COMMAND.

YES, GENERAL-SAN.

SHHLRIIP

I REMAIN.
TWHACK

I REMAIN TO FACE THE MACHINES.

28 JULY.

GENOA, ITALY.

LISTEN UP!

HOLD ONTO YOUR WEAPON, YOUR HELMET AND YOUR PACK!

MAKE SURE YOUR DUFFELS ARE LABELED WITH YOUR FULL NAME, UNIT AND AN ADDRESS IN THE STATES!

YOU WILL BE GIVEN YOUR ASSIGNED BERTHS IN THE ORDER THAT YOU BOARD!

THINK YOU'LL EVER SEE THAT DUFFEL AGAIN, HARV?
WHY NOT? I PUT MY NAME ON IT.
HA!

THOSE SWABBIES ARE GONNA HAVE A FIELD DAY WITH OUR GOODS.
RODRIGUEZ IS RIGHT. I GOT SIX BOTTLES OF VINO I KNOW I'M NEVER GONNA SEE AGAIN.

AW, YOU GUYS...
THEM SWABBIES WON'T BOTHER WITH THE LACE TABLECLOTH I GOT FOR MA.
LACE TABLECLOTH?
YOU GET HER SOME DOILIES TOO?

MY MA LIKES DOILIES.
DOWN, BIG FELLA.
STRUCK US FUNNY, IS ALL.

YOU GUYS BETTER SAVE IT FOR THE JAPS.

THE MIYAZAKI REGION ON KYUSHU IS THE STEP-OFF FOR OLYMPIC.
WITH A SECONDARY LANDING AT KUSHIKINO.

29 JULY.
USS MISSOURI, IN THE LUZON STRAIT.
MIYAZAKI IS A LONG SHORELINE WITH FLAT TERRAIN INLAND.
WE SECURE THE SOUTH TO GIVE THE AIR CORPS THEIR AIRSTRIPS TO STRIKE AT HONSHU.

LEM, YOUR MARINES WILL TAKE THE LEAD AND MY ARMY BOYS WILL DRIVE INLAND ON WAVE TWO.
WE'LL GET YOU YOUR BEACHHEADS, GENERAL.
THIS IS HARD DUTY, GENTLEMEN.

WE'RE LOOKING AT OVER A HUNDRED THOUSAND DEAD BEFORE THIS BLOODY MESS IS OVER.
AND THOSE POOR DAMNED JAPS?
A MILLION OR MORE OF THEM WILL BE REJOINING BUDDHA.

FOURTH QUARTER AND WE'RE ON THEIR TEN. RIGHT, CHUCK?
I'D SAY THIS WAS A LOT CLOSER TO HALF-TIME, GENERAL.

THE JAPS KNOW THE LANDING IS COMING AT KYUSHU.
AND SURE AS LITTLE APPLES THEY KNOW WE HAVE TO WAIT UNTIL AFTER TYPHOON SEASON.

YOU HAVE A POINT, CHUCK. MAKE IT.
THAT LAND OFF MIYAZAKI IS A FLOOD PLAIN. FLAT AS A PAN.
TANK COUNTRY.

IT'S A BIG AREA OF OPERATION.
YOU'LL NEED THE ARMY'S BEST OPEN COUNTRY ARMOR MAN.
DAMN IT, CHUCK.

DON'T SAY IT, CHUCK!
I DON'T WANT TO HEAR HIS NAME UNTIL I ABSOLUTELY HAVE TO!

29
JULY.
USS TRANSPORT PRIDE OF BALTIMORE.
SUEZ CANAL.
THEY'RE NOT ALL DAMN SAMURAIS, YOU KNOW...

MOST OF THE JAPS ARE PEASANTS. NO BETTER THAN FEUDAL SERFS.
AND THIS TALK ABOUT BUSHIDO IS A LOAD OF CRAP. WHAT THE HELL GOOD IS SUICIDAL COURAGE?

GIVE ME A MAN FIGHTING TO STAY ALIVE OVER ONE WILLING TO DIE ANY DAY OF THE WEEK.
WHAT ABOUT THOSE BANZAI CHARGES, GENERAL PATTON?
HUH.

THE ONLY THING I'M WORRIED ABOUT--
--IS HOSING THOSE LITTLE YELLOW BASTARDS OUT OF THE TREADS OF MY TANK.

30 JULY.

THE NAGASAKI PREFECTURE.

"AND THEY BROUGHT YOUNG CHILDREN TO HIM, THAT HE SHOULD TOUCH THEM.

"AND HIS DISCIPLES REBUKED THOSE THAT BROUGHT THEM.

AUGUST 1945.
OFF BAJA CALIFORNIA.
IT'S NOT GOING TO LAST **FOREVER.**
I KNOW, PAPA. I KNOW.

I HAVE AN OFFER FROM **RKO** FOR A COMEDY AND--
THIS ISN'T ABOUT YOUR **CAREER,** DAMMIT!
DO YOU WANT TO BE THOUGHT OF AS A COWARD?

AW, PAPA, YOU KNOW YOU'RE THE **ONLY** ONE I'D TAKE THAT FROM.
WELL. YOU'RE **GOING** TO HAVE TO TAKE IT FROM THE WHOLE DAMNED COUNTRY.
WHY HOLD YOUR MANHOOD CHEAP?

THAT'S FROM SHAKESPEARE.
YOU **KNOW** WHAT YOU HAVE TO DO.
STOP TRYING TO **EDUCATE** ME. WE'RE FISHING.
YEAH...

AND WHO MUST WE THANK FOR THIS, CHILDREN?*
FATHER DANNY!
YES! FATHER DANNY!

NO. NO.
WE MUST THANK THE LORD. THIS BOUNTY IS HIS TO GRANT US.

AUGUST 1945
NAGASAKI PREFECTURE, JAPAN.
ALL THINGS COME FROM HIM AS ALL THINGS RETURN TO HIM.

ON THE TRUCK!
ALL CHILDREN ARE TO BOARD THE TRUCK.
*TRANSLATED FROM JAPANESE.

WHAT IS THIS ABOUT?
THESE CHILDREN ARE IN MY CARE.
NO LONGER! THEY ARE TO BE TRANSPORTED. IT IS A DIRECTIVE FROM THE EMPEROR HIMSELF.

ALL JAPANESE ARE TO SERVE IN THE DEFENSE OF THE HOMELAND.
THERE ARE NO EXCEPTIONS!
I MUST PROTEST--

WHAK
NO!
NO PROTEST!

FATHER DANNY--?
WATCH OVER THE CHILDREN AS BEST YOU CAN, SISTER.
I WILL PRAY FOR YOU.

AND I WILL PRAY FOR JAPAN.

WHAT'S TRUE, HARV?
WHAT THEM SWABBIES IS SAYIN'. THAT WE'RE SHIPPIN' FOR THE PACIFIC.
SCUTTLEBUTT.

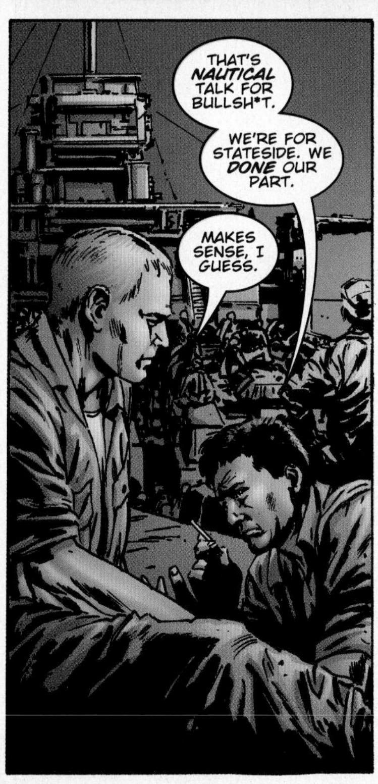

12 AUGUST.
FLEMISH CAP.
NORTH ATLANTIC.
DAMN IT ALL. WHERE ARE THEY?*

FLOATING HERE IN THE DARK.
NOT CARING IF WE GET A TORPEDO UP THE ASS.

THERE, HERR CAPITAN!

HASTE, GENTLEMEN. WE ARE EXPOSED HERE.
MAKE CERTAIN YOU HAVE ALL YOU NEED WITH YOU.
*TRANLATED FROM GERMAN.

CASTING LINES!
SECURE BOW AND AFT!
GET THAT GEAR STOWED AND THOSE MEN BELOW!
AYE, SIR!
WE ARE AWAY IN ONE MINUTE!
CAREFUL WITH THAT CASE!
GERMANS DIED TO GET IT THIS FAR!

WELCOME ABOARD U-TWO-SEVENTEEN, PROFESSORS.
I HOPE WE CAN MAKE YOU COMFORTABLE.

IT WILL BE A LONG JOURNEY FOR ALL OF US.
AND A HISTORICAL ONE, CAPITAN.
IF OUR NIPPONESE FRIENDS HAVE NOT MISLED US.

NAME.

WAYNE.

THAT *IS* MY LAST NAME.

YOUR *LAST* NAME, CLABBERHEAD.

JESUS PALOMINO.

1 SEPTEMBER.
ISLAND OF KYUSHU.
WHAT'S THE DESIGNATION, COLLEGE?
CADILLAC BEACH. THEY'RE ALL NAMED AFTER CARS.

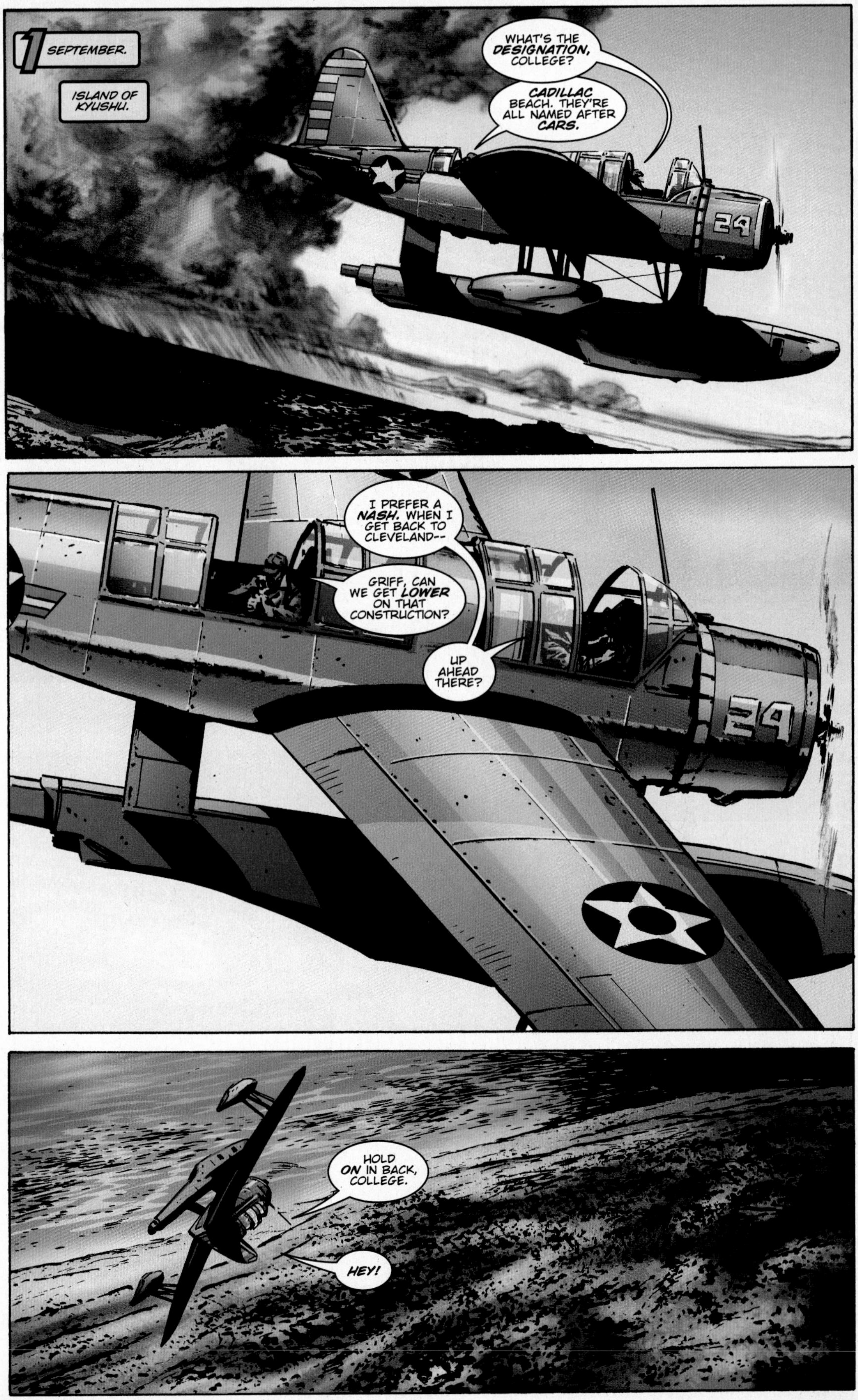

I PREFER A NASH. WHEN I GET BACK TO CLEVELAND--
GRIFF, CAN WE GET LOWER ON THAT CONSTRUCTION?
UP AHEAD THERE?

HOLD ON IN BACK, COLLEGE.
HEY!

THERE'S *MILES* OF TRENCHES.
EVERY JAP IN *CREATION* IS DOWN THERE DIGGIN'.

BLAM!
CRACK!
AND THE ONLY SHOOTIN' BACK WE CAN DO IS WITH THAT *BROWNIE* OF YOURS.
KPOW
KPOW
KRACK!

UNNH! *DAMN,* GRIFF!
SHE'S NOT BUILT FOR *COMFORT,* COLLEGE.

THEY ARE GONE!*
BACK TO WORK!
KPOW
PKKOW
POW
BLAMM

THE AMERICANS COME SOON!
THEY WILL BLEED AND THEY WILL BURN AND THEY WILL FALL!
TWAK!
WHACK!

THE HOMELAND WILL BE SOAKED IN THEIR BLOOD!
NOT ONE MAY LIVE TO LEAVE THIS BEACH!

WE ARE LIKE THE PETALS OF THE ROSE!
SO THE EMPEROR COMMANDS!
*TRANSLATED FROM JAPANESE

SAME DAY.
USS NEW JERSEY.
AT ANCHOR 20 MILES N/NW OF OKINAWA.
HIT THE LIGHTS, WILLYA?

I WAS RIGHT, GRIFF. THOSE WERE WOMEN AND KIDS DOWN THERE.
DIGGING SLIT TRENCHES AND BUNKERS.

AND THESE CONCRETE VIADUCTS.
THESE LOOK LIKE FUEL LINES.

THOSE SORRY BASTARDS ON X-DAY.
THIS IS GOING TO MAKE IWO LOOK LIKE A PICNIC.
I FLEW STRAFING MISSIONS ON IWO, COLLEGE.

THIS IS GONNA MAKE HELL LOOK LIKE A PICNIC.

Welcome
TO
JAPAN
NOW
UNDER NEW
MANAGEMENT

20
OCTOBER 1945.
"SHIMBU-TAI" BRIGADE, 4TH DIVISION, HOME AIR ARMY.
"COVERED WITH THE FLOWERS, INSTANTLY I'D LIKE TO DIE IN THIS DREAM OF OURS." ETSUJIN (1656-1739)

"I FLY FROM KAGOSHIMA FIELD TO STRIKE AT THE GAIJIN INVADERS.*
*TRANSLATED FROM THE JAPANESE.

"SONGS OF FAREWELL AND SONGS OF UNDYING GLORY ARE SUNG FOR US.

"I THINK OF YOU AND OUR CHILD AND THIS GIVES ME COURAGE.

"WE WILL NOT RETURN. WE WENT WILLINGLY AND EVEN EAGERLY.

"MY LIFE WAS NOTHING WHEN MEASURED AGAINST FATE.
"IT WAS WORTH THE NUMBER OF ENEMY LIVES THAT I MIGHT TRADE FOR IT.
"AND NO MORE.
"PRAY THAT MY HAND WAS STEADY IN THE FINAL MOMENTS.
"AS I PRAY FOR YOU AND OUR CHILD.

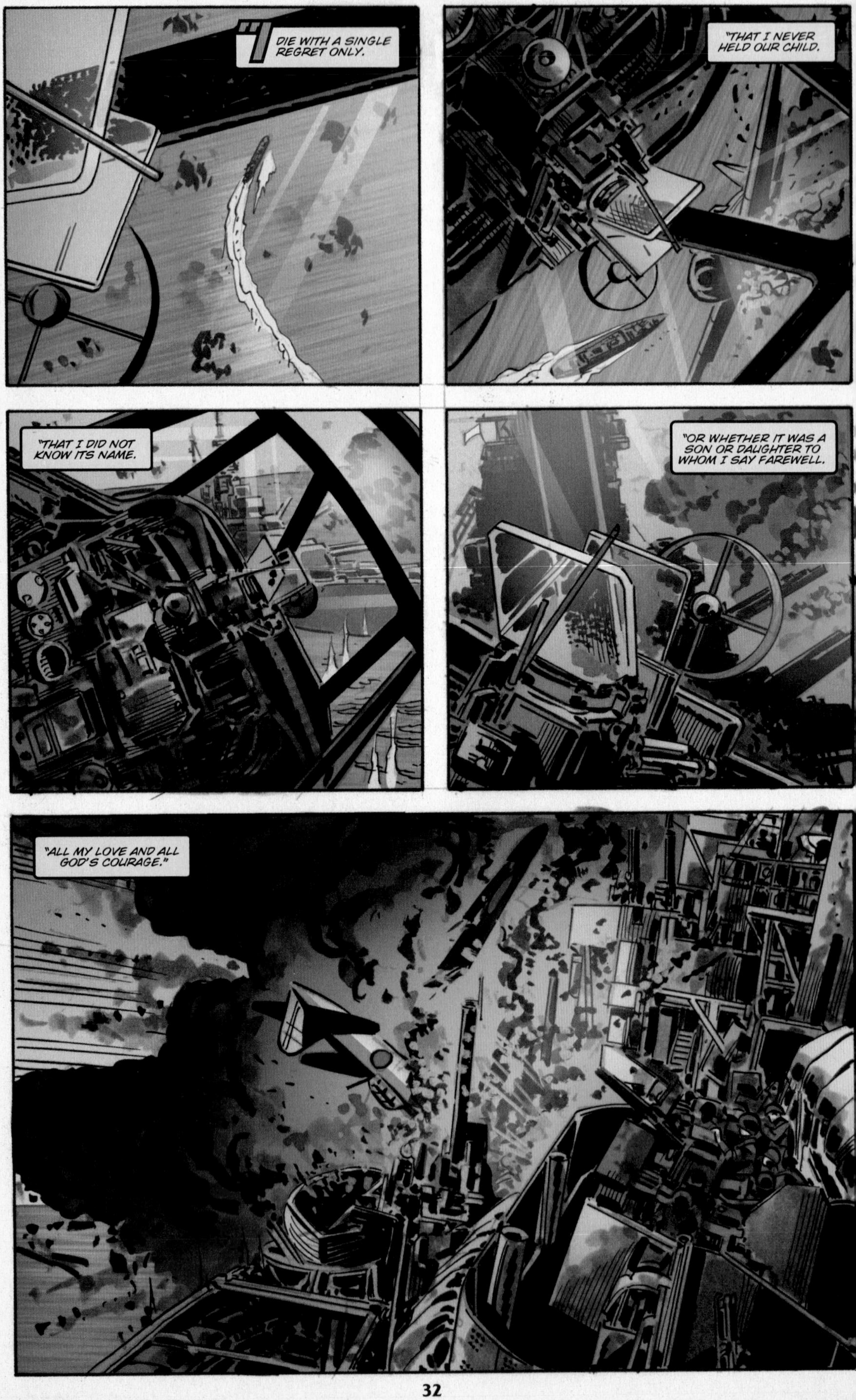

"ALL MY LOVE AND ALL GOD'S COURAGE."

29 OCTOBER.
OSUMI STRAIT.
SECOND BATTALION!
LISTEN UP!

THE 92ND HAS ITS ORDERS FOR "X" DAY.
WE WILL BE LANDING ON BEACH DESIGNATE CADILLAC ONCE THE BEACH IS SECURED BY THE JARHEADS.
WE'RE PART OF THE INLAND PUSH IN CONJUNCTION WITH THIRD ARMORED.

YOU'LL ALL BE GETTING ONE OF THESE.
MAKE SURE YOU LEARN IT IF YOU WANT TO MAKE TIME WITH ANY MAMA-SANS LANDSIDE.

HELL, WE WERE SUPPOSED TO BE HOME BY NOW.
DON'T WORRY SO MUCH, RODRIGUEZ.
AND WHY NOT, HARV?
THEY'RE BOMBIN' THAT BEACH DAY AND NIGHT--

--ALLA THEM JAPS ARE DEAD BY NOW.
JESUS, GUYS--

IT'S A DAMN JAP!
WE GOT A QUIZ KID HERE.
YOU GUYS FIFTH PLATOON?
WE'RE THIRD SQUAD OF THE FIFTH.

I'M 442ND. BUT THEY BROKE US UP, SO EVERY UNIT HAS A TRANSLATOR.
I NEED TO REPORT TO YOUR C.O.

LIEUTENANT MEYERS IS THAT FELLA WITH THE GLASSES OVER THERE.
I OWE YOU ONE. TAKE IT EASY.
WE'LL TAKE IT ANY WAY WE CAN, MOTO.

SEEMS LIKE A NICE ENOUGH GUY.
GET BACK TO ME WHEN HE'S SLIPPED A KNIFE IN YOUR BACK.
YOU'RE AS DUMB AS YOU ARE BIG, HARV.

1 NOVEMBER.
CITY OF NAGASAKI.

IT IS A WHITE MAN. HE ASKED FOR YOUR DEATH PRAYER.*
LAST RITES, THEY'RE CALLED.
IS HE *ENGLISH*, THEN?
*TRANSLATED FROM THE JAPANESE.

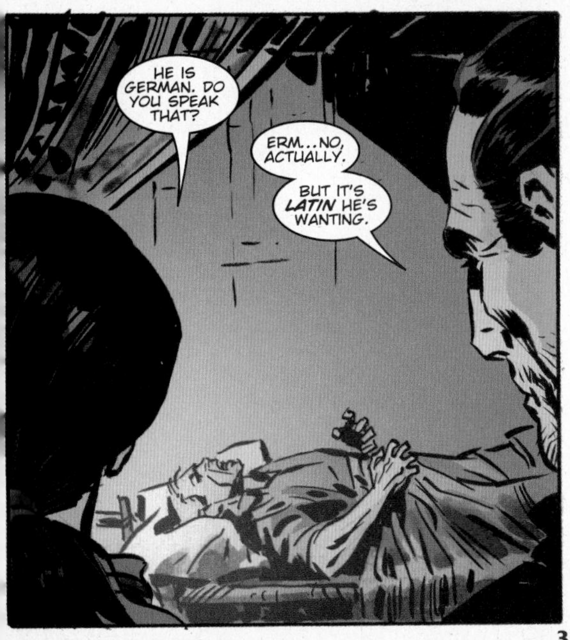

HE IS GERMAN. DO YOU SPEAK THAT?
ERM...NO, ACTUALLY.
BUT IT'S *LATIN* HE'S WANTING.

IS HE WOUNDED?
A RUPTURED APPENDIX. WE COULD DO NOTHING FOR HIM.
LIEBER GOTT--HILFT MIR, GOTT

YOU HAD BETTER HURRY.
YES. I SUPPOSE.

WENN-- WENN UNS OBERFLACHE TUN?
OBERFLACHE? SURFACE?

SIE SIND EIN SUBSEEMANN, JA?
JA--IM U-217--ZWEI JAHRE--
WARUM SIND SIE IN JAPAN?

ORDNUNGEN--EINIGE WISSENSCHAFTLER AN BORD--
SCIENTISTS?
WELCHER WISSENSCHAFTLER, MEIN SOHN?

ICH KENNE NICHT-- ICH--
GOTT-- ICH KANN NICHT SIE SEHEN

PER ISTAM SANCTAM UNCTIONEM ET--

WE NEED HIS BED.
OH!

--ET SUAM PIISSIMAM MISERICORDIAM, INDULGEAT TIBI DOMINUS--

YOU ARE ENGLISH?
I'M AN IRISHMAN. BUT I SPEAK ENGLISH.
MY DAUGHTER IS LEARNING ENGLISH IN SCHOOL.

THERE IS LITTLE TO PLEASE A CHILD IN THE WORLD THESE DAYS.
RIGHT ENOUGH, DOCTOR-SAN.
I AM MATSOSHI ISEYA.

DANIEL MONAGHAN.
I WOULD BE PLEASED IF YOU WOULD JOIN MY FAMILY FOR DINNER, DANIEL-SAN.
THIS EVENING?

AND I WOULD BE HONORED.
I THANK YOU FOR MY DAUGHTER.
I WILL ENDEAVOR TO ENTERTAIN HER.

12 NOVEMBER.
CV-15 USS RANDOLPH.

YOU SEE THAT?
HOW COULD I MISS IT, BARNSIE?

ANOTHER JAP GOES TO BUDDHA.
AND TAKES A CARRIER WITH HIM.
COULDA BEEN US.

CLEAR THE DECK!
YOU TOURISTS GET YOUR ASSES BELOW!

WHAT MAKES THEM DO THAT, JIMMY?
WHO DO WHAT, HARV?
THEM KAMO-KAZIE PILOTS RAMMIN' THOSE SHIPS.
HOW THE HELL SHOULD I KNOW?

YOU BEIN' JAPANESE AND ALL.
I WASN'T RAISED TO BE A SAMURAI.
ALL I WANTED WAS TO GROW UP AND PITCH FOR THE CARDINALS.

YOU YANKEE NO JAPPY, EH?
WHEN WE GET ON THAT BEACH YOU'RE A NIP NO MATTER WHERE YOUR MA SQUIRTED YOU OUT.

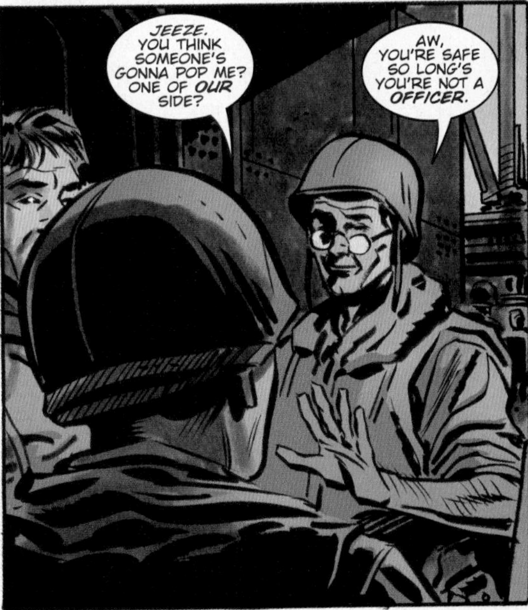
JEEZE. YOU THINK SOMEONE'S GONNA POP ME? ONE OF OUR SIDE?
AW, YOU'RE SAFE SO LONG'S YOU'RE NOT A OFFICER.

YOU ARE THE *INSTRUMENTS* OF THE EMPEROR'S FURY!

EACH OF YOU IS A HERO! *EACH* OF YOU IS ASSURED A HOME IN HEAVEN!

*TRANSLATED FROM THE JAPANESE.

YOU KNOW YOUR WEAPONS?
YES, TAITO-SAN!
YOUR ARMS ARE STRONG AND AIM IS KEEN?
YES, TAITO-SAN!

WITH SUCH WARRIORS, I KNOW THE HOMELAND IS SAFE.
YOU WILL TURN THE TIDES RED WITH GAIJIN BLOOD.

TO COVER!
TO COVER!

12 NOVEMBER.
X DAY PLUS SIX HOURS.
GOOD MORNING, GENTLEMEN.
YOU'RE LIVE, GENERAL, IN THREE... TWO...

TODAY WE TAKE THE FIRST STEPS IN THE FINAL BATTLE OF THIS WAR.
TODAY WE ATTACK THE ENEMY ON HIS HOME ISLANDS.

WE HAVE WAITED AND PRAYED FOR THIS DAY TO COME.
AND I AM CERTAIN YOU WILL ALL ACQUIT YOURSELF WITH COURAGE, HONOR AND--

--DEDICATION.
WHAT'RE YOU DOIN', JIMMY?
A SWABBIE LENT ME SOME *PAINTS*.

THE RED, WHITE AND BLUE, FRONT AND BACK.
I'M FROM TOPEKA, NOT TOKYO, AND EVERY-ONE SHOULD KNOW THAT.

YOUR LITTLE YELLOW COUSINS ON THE BEACH'LL SEE THAT A MILE AWAY.
SO LONG AS I'M SAFE FROM MY BROTHERS IN GREEN, RODRIGUEZ.

SEASICK OR THE JITTERS, WADDY?

FIVE PLATOON! TOP SIDE!
DAMN.

GOT A DEAL FOR YOU, BARNSIE--

--YOU CARRY MY GEAR TODAY AND I'LL CARRY YOURS TOMORROW.
MY LUCK I GET KILLED AND YOU'RE IN CLOVER.
THEM MARINES IS CATCHIN' HELL OVER THERE.

WE WERE SUPPOSED TO JUMP OFF HOURS AGO.
MUSTA RUN INTO MORE THAN THEY EXPECTED, HUH?
I DUNNO, HARV. WHO KNOWS WHAT WE'RE UP AGAINST?

THIS YOUR FIRST TIME HERE?
SWEDEN? NEVER BEEN THERE.
YOU EVER BEEN TO WHERE YOUR FOLKS ARE FROM?
IT AIN'T GONNA BE NO HOMECOMING FOR ME, EITHER.

ON YOUR FEET, YOU WEAK-KNEED SONS OF BITCHES!
GUNS UP! FIRE YOUR WEAPONS!

BANZAI!

CORPSMAN!

CORPSMAN, DAMN IT!
I AM FRIGHTENED, ISHI.

OUR FATHER IS DEAD. OUR MOTHER IS DEAD. OUR SISTERS ARE DEAD.
NOW IT IS OUR TURN TO DIE, EKU.
YES.

THERE IS NO FEAR FOR US!
YES! WE ARE HEROES!
THE WEAPON OF THE EMPEROR!
WE ARE HIS FURY!

AMEKO EADA SHEE!

AMEKO EADA SHEE AMEKO EADA SHEE!!

EEH!
EKU!

EKU...
YOU GO TO MOTHER AND FATHER.

I FIGHT ALONE, NOW.

WHAT WAS THIS LITTLE BASTARD SCREAMIN'?
"AMERICANS EAT SH*T."
ONLY ENGLISH HE'S EVER GONNA LEARN.

STE
UNIO
A. N. WILLIAMS
PRESIDENT
WASHINGTON DC 26
DEC 26
DEEP REGRET
REPORTED
IF FURTHER
WILL BE
WAR DESIRES
HUSBAND PRIVATE
IN ACTION SINCE
OR OTHER
PROMPTLY NOTIFIED
DUNLOP ACTING
Leona
Chicago

11 DECEMBER 1945.
TOKYO PREFECTURE.
WHUMP
WHAM
VROOOM!
KARUMP
WHEEEEEEEEEE
WHRAMM!

THOSE POOR DAMNED JAPS...
BUTCH GUICE

LIKE A FURNACE DOWN THERE.
FIGURES, RIGHT? ALLA THEM PAPER HOUSES.

WE HIT A STOCKYARD?
I'M SMELLIN' STEAK UP HERE.
YOU'RE GOOFY, STUBBS.

THAT'S JAPS COOKIN' OFF.
TOKYO'S ONE BIG BARBECUE TONIGHT.

HWOOP!
OH JESUS...

RRMMMRRRRRRRMMMMMMMMRRRRMMMM
THOSE POOR DAMNED JAPS...
DO CASTLE, RESIDENCE OF THE IMPERIAL EMPEROR.

WHUMP
THE BUNKER OF THE MOST AUGUST GOD AND EMPEROR HIROHITO.
THE AMERICANS MUST BE MADE TO SUFFER.*
*TRANSLATED FROM THE JAPANESE.

OUR ONLY HOPE FOR JAPAN AND ITS PEOPLE LIES IN OUR RESOLVE.
BRUMMMMMMMMMMM

OUR WILL MUST REMAIN STRONG. OUR WILL MUST BE GREATER THAN THE INVADERS'.
IF IT IS NOT THEN WE WILL BE SLAVES OF THE AMERICANS. JAPAN WILL BE NO MORE.

IF ENOUGH AMERICAN BLOOD IS SPILT THEY WILL SEEK A NEGOTIATED PEACE.
UNDER THE TERMS OF SUCH A SURRENDER WE MAY RETAIN OUR HONOR. ANYTHING LESS IS UNACCEPTIBLE.
KABO
OOMMMM

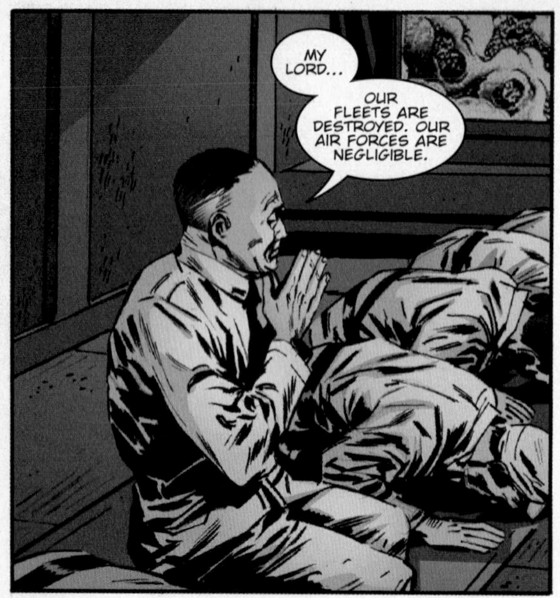
MY LORD...
OUR FLEETS ARE DESTROYED. OUR AIR FORCES ARE NEGLIGIBLE.

THEN YOU WILL ATTACK WITH WHAT YOU HAVE, ADMIRAL KONDO.
ATTACK. *ONLY* ATTACK.

WE BATTLE FOR OUR LIVES.
DEATH IS NOTHING. PAIN IS NOTHING.

SURVIVAL IS ALL. OUR FUTURE IS PARAMOUNT.

THRUM

AH!
BBRUUMMMMM

MY LORD--?

YOU WILL DO AS I SAY.
AH.

YOU WILL DRIVE OUR PEOPLE TO GREATER EFFORT.
BRWHOOMMM

YOU WILL NOT COMMIT SEPPUKU.
I WILL NO LONGER ALLOW THIS.

YOU WILL LIVE. YOU WILL COMMAND.

ATTACK.
ONLY ATTACK.

21 DECEMBER.
MIYAZAKI PREFECTURE, KYUSHU.
CLANKETY CLANKETY CLANKETY CLANKE

WE GOT ONE, HARV.
I SEE 'EM.
CLANK CLANK CLANK CLANK

KPOW
AMEKO DIE! DIE!
POW

HWAH!
SSSSSSSS
ZING
BEEOW

POW!
SSSSSSSSSSSSSSSS
POW!
POW
SH*#!

BLAAMG
SH*#!

WELL, TONTO--
LOOKS LIKE OUR WORK IS DONE HERE.
I THOUGHT I WAS THE LONE RANGER, RODRIGUEZ.

WHAT? THE MASKED MAN CAN'T BE A MEXICAN?
HE'S A TEXAN, DUMBASS. I'M A TEXAN.

HE'S FROM HOLLYWOOD, HARV. TWO RED CAR STOPS FROM MY HOUSE.

WE HEARD THAT BLAST, GUYS.
OUR TANK GOT EIGHT-SIXED, BARNSIE. BUT WE'RE STILL HERE.

HEY, YOU A NISEI TRANSLATOR?
THAT'S WHAT IT SAYS ON MY PAYCHECK.
A JAP BOB HOPE, EH? WE GOT WORK FOR YOU.

私達は
何も
言わない!

WE NEED TO KNOW THE CONDITION OF THE ROAD THROUGH TO SAGA.
I'LL SEE WHAT I CAN DO, SIR.

友人。
前方の道、
は採鉱され
るか。*
*THE ROAD AHEAD, FRIEND. IS IT MINED?

奴隷である
か。あなたの
球を手渡し
たか?*
*ARE YOU THEIR SLAVE? HAVE YOU SURRENDERED YOUR BALLS?

はあ私ア
メリカ
人である。な
たの生命を救
試ている*
*I AM AN AMERICAN. I AM TRYING TO SAVE YOUR LIFE.

PTOOO

BLAM!

私は話す!!
私は話す!!
THIS ONE SEEMS MORE TALKATIVE.

ANYTHING USEFUL?
THEY'VE FLOODED THE PADDIES FIVE MILES EAST OF HERE, SIR.
AND THERE'S ONE OF THOSE GASOLINE TRENCHES ACROSS THE FEEDER ROAD TO THE SOUTH.

OKAY, I SEE THAT. GOOD WORK.
WHAT WILL YOU DO WITH THE PRISONER, SIR?
DON'T WORRY ABOUT HIM. HE'LL BE TAKEN CARE OF.

KAPOW!

22 DECEMBER.
MITSUBISHI FACTORY, NAGASAKI PREFECTURE.
THERE!
THERE!

I CAN HEAR HIM.
HE IS THERE!

HAH!

ANOTHER FAT ONE!

I APOLOGIZE FOR THE PLAINNESS OF THIS MEAL...

THE RICE IS NOT OF THE BEST QUALITY.
MY SISTER IS AN EXCELLENT COOK AND DOES WHAT SHE CAN.
IT'S ALL APPRECIATED, I ASSURE YOU.

THANKING YOU, FATHER DANNY, FOR TAKING UNCLE'S INVITATION.
I LIKE VERY MUCH SPEAKING ENGLISH.
AND YOU SPEAK IT VERY WELL, FUMIKO.

I COULD STAND THE PRACTICE IN ENGLISH AS WELL, FATHER.
AND PERHAPS A PRIMER ON THE USE OF THESE STICKS, EH?

YOU ARE A DOCTOR ALSO, DR. GERLACH? WHAT AREA OF MEDICINE DO YOU PRACTICE?
AH, I AM NOT A PHYSICIAN. I AM A DOCTOR OF SCIENCE.

SIE SAGEN ZU VIEL, WALTER.
ER IST EIN PRIESTER, KURT.
SIE SORGEN SICH WIE EINE FRAU.

UNSERE ARBEIT KANN NICHT VON FREI GESPROCHEN WERDEN.
PHAH! ICH WERDE NICHT MEHR SAGEN.

ENGLISH ONLY, PLEASE!
I AM SORRY. MY ENGLISH IST SEHR SCHLECHT-- VERY POOR.

DON'T APOLOGIZE, DR. DIEBNER. I STRUGGLE TO BE BI-LINGUAL. MY JAPANESE IS ATROCIOUS.
IS IT NOT, MADAME HARUKO?

ENGLISH... SPEAK LITTLE, FATHER.
VERY SORRY.

YOU ARE AN ENGLANDER, FATHER?
I'M IRISH, DOCTOR. NOT A DROP OF ENGLISH BLOOD.

AND I SHARE NO SYMPATHIES WITH THEM, EITHER.
BY FAITH AND BY BIRTH I AM AN ENEMY OF THE CROWN, SIR.

SO, FATHER.
DOES YOUR PRESENCE IN JAPAN MAKE YOU UNWELCOME IN YOUR HOMELAND?

I DO GOD'S WORK NO MATTER WHERE I FIND MYSELF.
MOST OF MY COUNTRYMEN FEEL FOR THOSE OPPRESSED BY THE ENGLISH.

MANY IRISH REPATRIATED TO GERMANY TO JOIN THE WEHRMACHT.
WE SHARED MANY OF THE SAME GOALS, EH?

BUT SUCH A WEIGHTY TOPIC FOR YOUNG EARS, AND ALL.

I'M SURE FUMIKO WOULD RATHER SPEAK OF OTHER THINGS.

SHALL I TELL YOU ABOUT THE PONY I ONCE OWNED BACK IN SLIGO, THEN?
SIEH? SIE SORGEN SICH ZU VIEL.
WIR MÜSSEN VORSICHTIG SEIN.

I HAVE NOT HEARD HER LAUGH IN SO MANY MONTHS.

NOT SINCE HER FATHER WAS LAST HERE.
AND *HE*--?
GAVE HIS LIFE ON SAIPAN.

I AM GRATEFUL TO YOU...FOR *HER.*
EVEN FOR A *MOMENT'S* HAPPINESS IN THESE DAYS OF MISERY.

THEY WERE HAPPY MOMENTS FOR MYSELF AS WELL, MADAME HARUKO.
A CHILD'S LAUGHTER IS AS A *BALM* TO ME.

FATHER, THE *GERMANS* ARE RETURNING TO THE CITY. THEY WILL TAKE YOU BACK.
THANK YOU, ISEYA.
CAN I IMPLORE UPON YOU TO *RETURN* WHEN YOU MAY, FATHER?

I LOOK *FORWARD* TO IT WITH KEEN ANTICIPATION.

25 DECEMBER.
MERRY CHRISTMAS, YOU SAD, SAD BASTARDS.
DIXON'S DELI
GRUB FOR THE GRUBBY

THIS S'POSED TO BE TURKEY?
IT AIN'T BAD WITH ENOUGH SALT.

FOOD WAS BETTER IN ITALY.
HELL, EVERYTHING WAS BETTER THERE.

THEM FOLKS WAS GLAD TO SEE US.
DAMN STRAIGHT, KEMOSABE.
A FEW SMOKES, A FEW CHOCOLATE BARS AND THEM GUINEAS WERE OUR PALS.

HERE, EVERY NIP OUTTA DIAPERS IS LOOKIN' TO KILL US.
AND IN ITALY A GUY COULD GET LAID.

HA! HA! HA! HA! HA!
GET HIM!
YOU'RE A ROMANTIC, BARNSIE.

KRAK
OOH.

BWEEEEEE

AMEKO EADA SHEE!
SON OF A B*TCH.

SON OF A B*TCH!
SON OF A B*TCH!
DIXON'S
GRUB FOR THE GRUBBY
KPOW
POW

KPOW
POW
TZING

CLICK
DAMN IT!

SPLOCH
SWOP
SPOP
SPLOP
SPLOCH
SPLOOP

THWAK!
HUNH!

WHUMP
WHUMP
THUMP
CHUNK

WHAT GIVES WITH THESE JAPS? DON'T THEY KNOW WHEN THEY'RE LICKED?
DON'T THEY KNOW THEY'D BE IN CLOVER IF THEY'D JUST SURRENDER?
THEY'LL NEVER QUIT.

WE'RE GONNA HAVE TO KILL EVERY LAST MOTHER'S SON OF 'EM.
PERSONALLY? I'D GIVE MY RIGHT NUT TO STEP OVER THE BODY OF THE LAST JAP ON THE MAP.

31
DECEMBER.

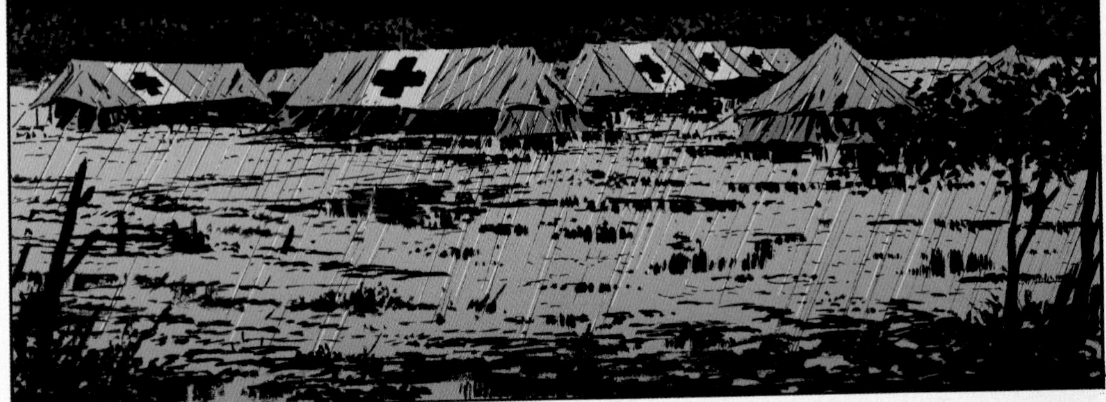
THE ROAD TO SAGA.

US NAVY MEDICAL CORPS.
145TH/108TH SURGICAL/EVACUATION HOSPITAL.
ABERNATHY AVENUE

DEAR GOD...

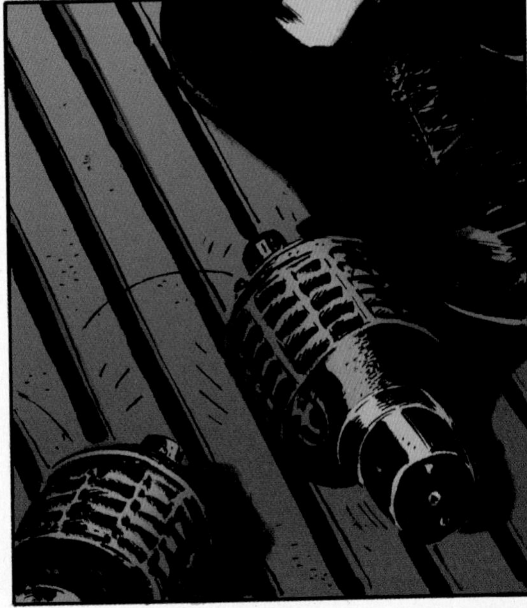

BLAM
WHUMP

--THE HELL?
THAT *KID*--

WHAAM

LITTLE BASTARD..!

THE BLOOD OF WARRIORS RUNS IN HIM!
OUR LITTLE BROTHER-- ISHI!

HE RAINS DEATH UPON THE EMPEROR'S ENEMIES!
ISHI-- GRENADE BOY!

ISHI-- GRENADE BOY!
ISHI-- GRENADE BOY!
ISHI-- GRENADE BOY!

GIVE 'EM HELL

*TRANSLATED FROM GERMAN

IN OUR EARLY EXPERIMENTS IN BERLIN--THE CALCULATIONS WERE OFF BY A FACTOR OF TEN.
NOW WE KNOW THAT A SUCCESSFUL ATOMIC REACTION DOES NOT REQUIRE SO MUCH PLUTONIUM.

AND THE BITTER IRONY IS THAT YOUR ARMY LACKS A HEAVY BOMBER.
THEY COULD NEVER CARRY EVEN OUR SMALLER MODEL OF HERMANN.

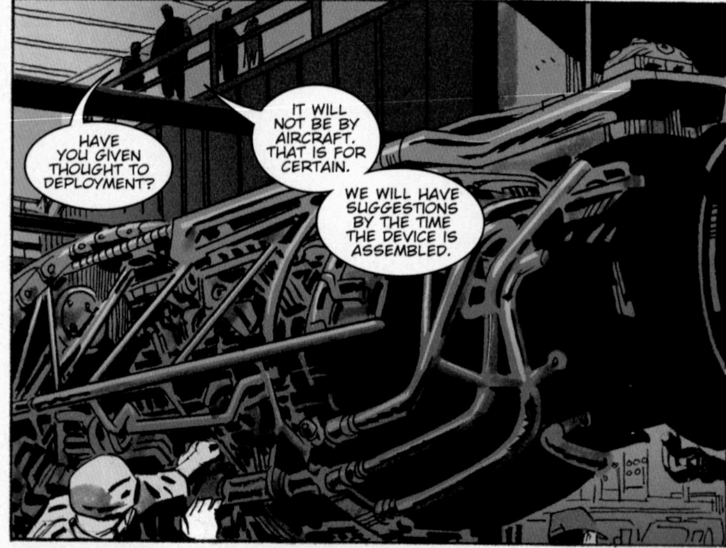
HAVE YOU GIVEN THOUGHT TO DEPLOYMENT?
IT WILL NOT BE BY AIRCRAFT. THAT IS FOR CERTAIN.
WE WILL HAVE SUGGESTIONS BY THE TIME THE DEVICE IS ASSEMBLED.

THE ADMIRAL RELAYS THE WISHES OF OUR EMPEROR.
IT IS HIS WISH THAT THE AMERICANS BE SUFFICIENTLY IMPRESSED WITH THIS WEAPON THAT THEY WILL ENTERTAIN A NEGOTIATED PEACE.

ASSURE YOUR EMPEROR IT WILL BE ALL OF THAT.

YOU WILL KEEP THE ADMIRAL INFORMED, PLEASE?
OF COURSE.
GOOD DAY, THEN.

THEY'RE *IMPATIENT,* WALTER.
UNDERSTANDABLE, NO? THIS COULD BE JAPAN'S LAST CHANCE AT A NEGOTIATED PEACE.

AND A *SLIM* CHANCE IT IS.
AN UNTESTED DEVICE. AN UNTESTED *THEORY.*

HERMANN? YOU *STILL* CALL IT THAT?
IT STILL REMINDS ME OF GOERING, KURT.
HA!

LIKE OUR FORMER REICHSMARSCHALL, IT IS TOO HEAVY TO GET ITS FAT ASS OFF THE GROUND.
HA HA!

1 JANUARY 1946.
EBINO FACTORY DISTRICT.
GOTTA TELL YOU, HARV--I DON'T LIKE THE IDEA OF SPENDING NEW YEARS WITH MARINES.
YOU CELEBRATE NEW YEARS, JIMMY?

WHY WOULDN'T I?
YOU BEIN' JAPANESE AND ALL.
THAT'S CHINESE NEW YEARS, YOU DUMB TEXAN.

THIS PLACE IS QUIET.
YEAH. I WANT TO GET US A PRISONER AND BACK TO THE CEE-PEE.

LEAVE THIS GUNG HO CRAP TO THE JARHEADS.

S**T THE BED...

IT'S A SNARE!
WITHDRAW!

UH.
KRAK!
DAMMIT!
SCHWALLY IS DOWN!

SNIPERS!
FIND COVER!

AW, WHY'D I VOLUNTEER TO COME WITH YOU?
WHY'D I LET MY PARENTS TEACH ME JAPANESE?

EADA SHEE!

POW!
GET YOUR ASSES OUDDA HERE!
I'LL SUPRESS THESE LITTLE BASTARDS!

AMEKO YOU DIE.
POW!
POW!
POW!

BBAROOMM

THE BIG DOPE'S STILL BREATHING.
WE CAN'T LEAVE HIM HERE.

GET DUKE BACK TO THE CORPSMEN!
NOW!
JENNINGS! BLOW THAT BARRICADE!

YO, GUNNY!

WHO IS *THERE?*

I HAVE *TRAVEL* PAPERS. I AM *AUTHORIZED* TO--
SHUT YOUR *MOUTH,* ENGLISH!

HE IS A *SPY!* BE *STILL,* ENGLISH!
THUNK!
WUNH!

HE IS *NOT* LYING, OHIRO!
HE *HAS* A PASS TO TRAVEL HERE!

I'M GLAD TO BE HEADIN' BACK--UNH--BUT WHY'D IT HAVE TO BE SUCH A BIG SUMB*TCH?
THIS JARHEAD NEVER--NFF--MISSED A CHOWLINE.

WELL, HE'S GOIN' HOME, HUH?

GOT WOUNDED HERE!
AID TENT'S THAT WAY. BUT THEY'RE FULL UP.
MP

WE'LL TAKE OUR CHANCES.
HOPE THEY GOT COFFEE GOIN'.

SOME HELP HERE?

LET'S GET A LOOK AT THAT FACE WOUND.

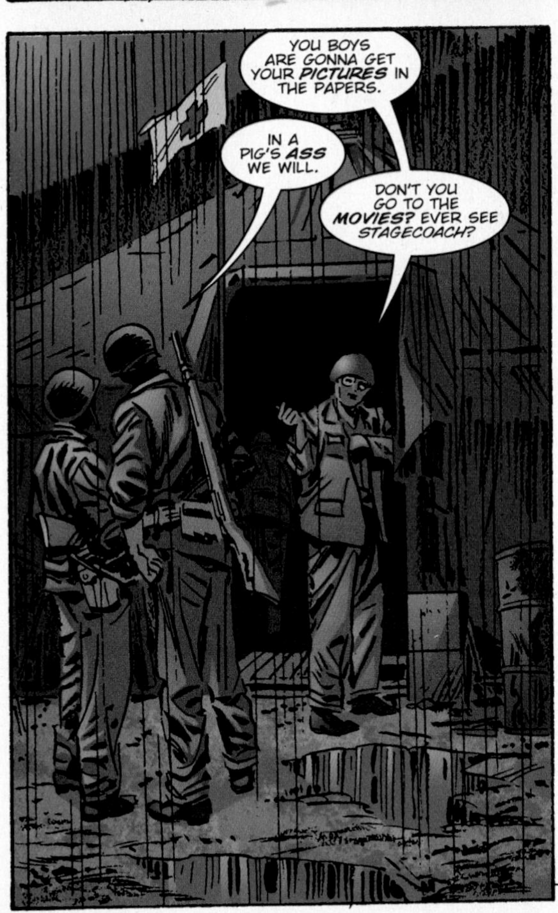
YOU BOYS ARE GONNA GET YOUR PICTURES IN THE PAPERS.
IN A PIG'S ASS WE WILL.
DON'T YOU GO TO THE MOVIES? EVER SEE STAGECOACH?

YOU JUST SAVED THE LIFE OF THE RINGO KID.

15 JANUARY.
THE FIFTH FLEET AT ANCHOR OFF NICHINAN.
I DON'T LIKE THIS ONE BIT.

TWO NAZI PHYSICISTS WE KNOW WERE IN THE GERMAN'S ATOMIC PROJECT.
AND THEY'RE COOLING THEIR HEELS IN NAGASAKI.

THINK THE JAPS ARE CLOSE TO A BOMB?
WITH THE HELP OF THESE KRAUTS THEY COULD BE.
OUR OP MISSED HIS LAST CHECK-IN.

IF HE'S STILL ALIVE, WE NEED HIM TO GET MORE.
HOW ARE THE JAPS TREATING THEM? HAVE THEY MENTIONED A DEPLOYMENT METHOD?

BRANG! BRANG! BRANG!
DAMN IT TO HELL.

ZEKE COMING IN HIGH!
GET A LEAD ON HIM!

PHOOM
PHOOM
PHOOM

...AND BLESSED IS THE FRUIT OF THY WOMB JESUS...

KRUMP!

VROOOSH!
ONE MEATBALL? THEY USUALLY COME IN DROVES.
SIR! TO AFT!

VOOSH
VOOSH
VROOSH

TAKKATAKKATAKKA!
帝国のための
百万の血!

WHAM!
VROOSH

11
JANUARY.
NAGASAKI PREFECTURE.
THE HOME OF DR. ISEYA.
YOU ARE INJURED, FATHER DANIEL?

A MISUNDERSTANDING, HARUKO.
IT SEEMS EVERY GAIJIN IS SUSPECT.
YOU SHOULD NOT TRAVEL ALONE, FATHER.

EXCELLENT ADVICE. BUT I MUST ATTEND TO MY CHURCH AND--
I WILL ACCOMPANY YOU THE NEXT TIME.
THAT'S VERY KIND OF YOU, HARUKO. BUT--

I WILL INSIST, FATHER. YOU ARE A WELCOME GUEST IN MY COUNTRY.
I ONLY WISH ALL OF YOUR PEOPLE SAW IT THAT WAY.

IF YOU WILL EXCUSE ME FOR A MOMENT.
OF COURSE.

SCHMUTZIGES WETTER. NICHT EIN RICHTIGER WINTER HIER.
SIE SIND NUR MIT UNSEREM FORTSCHRITT UNGEDULDIG.

FORTSCHRITT? KÖNNEN SIE ES DAS NENNEN?
DIE MÖGLICHKEITEN SIND HIER PRIMITIV. DIE JAPANER WISSEN NICHTS DER KERNDYNAMIK.

DA ZEIT ABLÄUFT, WÜRDE ICH EINEN ALTERNATIVEN GEBRAUCH UNSERER MATERIALIEN VORSCHLAGEN.
ICH BIN AUF JEDE LÖSUNG EIFRIG.

FATHER DANNY?
FUMIKO!

YOU DID NOT COME SEE ME.
IT IS VERY LATE. I DID NOT WISH TO--
IST JEMAND DORT?

I'LL SEE YOU BACK TO YOUR BED AND TELL YOU A STORY.
ABOUT IRELAND?
IF YOU LIKE.

12
JANUARY.
MAP REFERENCE K-111, KYOMACHI INDUSTRIAL AREA.
TURN YOUR HEAD A LITTLE TO THE LEFT...
THAT'S GOOD.

THIS FOR LIFE MAGAZINE?
I'M A STRINGER. COULD BE LIFE. OR COLLIERS.
SO YOU REALLY SAVED JOHN WAYNE'S LIFE?

ME AN' JIMMY CARRIED HIM TO AN AID STATION. DIDN'T KNOW WHO IT WAS TILL WE GOT HIM BACK.
YOU NEED A SHOT OF ME AN' JIMMY.

NAW. I GOT WHAT I NEED.
BUT JIMMY SHOULD BE IN THE PITCHER, TOO.
IT'S OKAY. I'LL MAKE SURE HE'S MENTIONED.

WHY WON'T YOU TAKE JIMMY'S PITCHER?
I GOT PLENTY PICTURES OF JAPS.
NOT THIS JAP.

MAN, THAT'S DIRTY WORK.
COULD BE ME DOWN THERE, BARNES.

KNOW WHAT YOU MEAN, JIMMY. MAYBE I'D RATHER BE FIGHTIN' 'EM THAN BURYIN' 'EM.
THAT'S NOT WHAT I MEANT.
LIME

IF MY GRANDPARENTS DIDN'T MOVE TO KANSAS--
--I COULDA BEEN GETTING LIME SPREAD OVER ME RIGHT NOW.

YEAH. IF MY MOM DIDN'T LEAVE POLAND WHO KNOWS WHAT WOULDA HAPPENED TO YOURS TRULY?
WE'RE LUCKY. THEY'RE NOT. TRY NOT TO TAKE IT PERSONAL.

TROUBLE, HARV?
NOTHIN' I CARE TO TALK ABOUT.

BRRRUMMM
BUT AS SOON'S I GET TO A FPO...
...I'M CANCELIN' MY SUBSCRIPTION TO LIFE.

VVVVVVVVRRRRRRRRRRRRRRRMMMMMM
22 JANUARY.
THE SKIES SOUTH OF KUMAMOTO.
RIO ONE TO RIO SQUAD--

--WE'RE SEEKING TARGETS OF OPPORTUNITY.
SING OUT IF YOU SEE ANYTHING SWEET. OVER.
ROGER, RIO ONE--

GRIFF, LOOK SEVEN O'CLOCK.
THE ROAD RUNNING SOUTH.
TAP TAP

VVVVVVVVVRRRRRRRRRREEEENNNNNN
EYES LIKE A HAWK THERE, COLLEGE.
RIO ONE TO SQUAD-- ROLL OUT ON ME.

WWWWEEEEENNNNN
飛行機!
KRAKOOMM
BROOM

RIO TO YANKEE CLIPPER-- STRUCK JAP TRAFFIC.
ROAD DESIGNATE A-9, TWENTY MILES NORTH ATSUSHIRO.

VVVVRRRRRRRRNNNNN
YANKEE CLIPPER HERE. STRENGTH ESTIMATE, RIO?
WE STUNG 'EM HARD BUT THERE'S MILES OF TRANSPORTS.

THEY'RE MOVIN' SOUTH AND THEY'RE MAD ABOUT SOMETHING. RIO OUT.
ROGER THAT, RIO.

GENERAL--
WE *HEARD*, DOMINIC.
PRAY THE WEATHER HOLDS.

'24 JANUARY 1946.

KYOMACHI IN THE SENDAI RIVER VALLEY.

KABOOMM

"HOW'D YOU LIKE THAT, GENERAL?"

I LIKED IT *FINE,* CHIP.

A DAMNED *TURKEY* SHOOT IS WHAT THIS IS. JAPS HAVEN'T *DEVELOPED* NEW ARMOR SINCE 1939.

THEY NEVER EXPECTED A *TANK* WAR IN THEIR OWN BACKYARD.

GENERAL PATTON, YOU REALLY SHOULDN'T BE OUT HERE.

AND WHERE THE HELL SHOULD I BE, JACK?
SO LONG AS IT'S PISSING DOWN RAIN THE DAMN AIR CORPS HAS TO SIT ON ITS ASS.

THIS DIVISON--MY DIVISION--IS THE ONLY THING BETWEEN THE JAPS AND EBINO.
I AM NOT ABOUT TO GO TO DOUG MacARTHUR AND TELL HIM HOW I HAD TO GIVE BACK THREE WEEKS OF HARD FIGHTING.

WON'T GIVE THE SON OF A B*TCH THE SATISFACTION, JACK.
I'M ONLY SUGGESTING THAT STANDING IN THE PATH OF A MAJOR COUNTER-OFFENSIVE MIGHT NOT BE THE BEST USE OF YOUR TALENTS, SIR.

THAT MAKES ALL THE SENSE IN THE WORLD.
BUT THERE'S NO PLACE ELSE I'D RATHER BE, JACK.

BANZAAAAAAAAAiiii

24 JANUARY 1946.
KYOMACHI IN THE SENDA RIVER VALLEY.
SPEARPOINTS GLEAMING. THE SHRIEK OF THEIR WAR ELEPHANTS RENDS THE AIR.
TWO ARMIES MEET AND ONE WILL FALL ON THE SANDS AT ZAMA.

"AND SO AN EMPIRE DIES."
GOT MORE AMMO FOR THE FIFTY, GENERAL!
NO GOOD, SON! BARREL'S RUINED!
FROM HERE ON IT'S ONE BULLET AT A TIME!

ONE JAP AT A TIME!

EIGHT KILOMETERS WEST.
THE ARMY IS GENEROUS IN DEATH. AN EMPTY BELLY IS BEST FOR FIGHTING.*
THEY KNOW THEY WILL EITHER DIE THIS DAY--
*TRANSLATED FROM THE JAPANESE.
--OR, VICTORIOUS, THEY WILL FEED ON AMERICAN RATIONS BY NIGHTFALL.
EITHER WAY, GLORY IS THEIRS.

UNCOOKED RICE. I AM NOT A BEGGAR, TAITO-SAN.
YOU NEED YOUR STRENGTH, ISHI. A WEAK ARM CANNOT THROW A GRENADE.
I WILL MOVE IN *CLOSER,* THEN.
A WARRIOR'S HEART FEEDS ONLY ON COURAGE, EH?
OUR SOLDIERS RUSH TO MEET THE ENEMY. THEIR HEARTS ARE STRONG.
THE AMERICANS THINK ONLY OF THEIR BELLIES. ONLY OF THEIR COMFORT.
A SAMURAI REJECTS THESE THINGS. HE LOOKS TO ETERNITY.
HE KNOWS THIS DAY WILL BE REMEMBERED FOREVER.
I DO NOT WISH TO DIE. I WISH TO KILL. FOR MY FAMILY. FOR JAPAN.
FOR MYSELF.
A MOTOR.

STAY ON AIMING POINT. WILL RECON SOLO. CHECK?
COLLEGE--
ROGER, RIO LEADER.
--WANNA SEE HOW LOW THE WEATHER CEILING IS?
COULD BE CLOUDS OVER HIGHWAY NINE OR FOG OVER MOUNT KUROMI.
RIO ONE TO RIO SQUAD.
TARGET AREA SOCKED IN.
EITHER WAY, GRIFF--
--WE'LL NEVER SEE IT COMING.
THAT'S IT, KID.
KEEP LOOKIN' AT THE SUNNY SIDE.

RIO ONE TO RIO SQUAD.
CEILING THREE HUNDRED FEET.

SENDAI RIVER ROAD--HIGHWAY DESIGNATE NINE--LOTS OF TRAFFIC MOVING EAST.
TARGETS OF OPPORTUNITY. TRUCKS AND LOTS OF JAPS.

COLLEGE?
ANSWER ME, KID!
ISHI-- LEAVE ME--
I WILL NOT. YOU WILL LIVE TO FIGHT.
PLEASE--
THE RICE, TAITO SAN--
UHH?
IT IS COOKED NOW.

THIRD FLEET.
USS LEXINGTON.
OSUMI-KAIKYU STRAIT.

CORPSMAN! GET A CORPSMAN!
WE HAVE WOUNDED!
DON'T TOUCH HIM! NO ONE TOUCH HIM!

COLLEGE...
...I'M SO DAMNED SORRY...

...

26 JANUARY.
NAGASAKI PREFECTURE.
YOU TAKE A TREMENDOUS RISK, HARUKO.

NOT AS MUCH AS YOURSELF, FATHER DANIEL. A WHITE MAN TRAVELING ALONE IS IN DANGER.
YOU HAVE MY THANKS.

THE CHURCH IS UNSTABLE. I'LL GO IN ALONE.
THERE ARE PARISH RECORDS IN THE SACRISTY THAT I CANNOT LEAVE BEHIND.

I WILL BE ONLY A MOMENT.

FATHER DANIEL?

THERE ARE SOLDIERS AND...
...SCIENTISTS PRESENT HERE FROM PROJECT IN BERLIN...

DO YOU HAVE A CURRENT LOCATION FOR THEM, SLINGSHOT?
NOT FOR THREE DAYS, ARROWHEAD. I BELIEVE THEY ARE MAKING FINAL PREPARATIONS FOR DEPLOY-MENT.

THAT WOULD PLACE THEM SOMEWHERE IN NAGASAKI PORT AREA.
A SUBMARINE SLIP OR OTHER DEEP ANCHORAGE.
OH.

HARUKO.
YOU ARE NO PRIEST.
THAT'S RIGHT, HARUKO. I'M NOT EVEN IRISH.
I'M WITH BRITISH INTELLIGENCE.

YOU MUST UNDERSTAND. I DO WHAT I DO TO END THIS WAR. I WANT TO SAVE LIVES.
I HAVE LIVED HERE TEN YEARS AND HAVE AN AFFECTION FOR THE JAPANESE.

FOR YOU, HARUKO.
DO YOU SEE THE TRUTH IN MY EYES?

SPY!*
*TRANSLATED FROM THE JAPANESE.

SPY!
THIS MAN SPIES FOR THE ENGLISH!

HE HAS TRICKED ME INTO BRINGING HIM HERE!

THEN HE DIES.
KILL HIM.

NO! I THOUGHT YOU WOULD ARREST HIM!
I WILL ARREST YOU FOR CONSORTING WITH A SPY.
NO!

TRAITOR!

CUT OFF.
I'VE HEARD ENOUGH. WE GO TO FLEET.

27 JANUARY.
HELP ME, ISHI--
--TO FOLLOW MY GENERAL--
--IN HONOR--
YOU LOST YOUR SWORD ON THE ROAD, TAITO-SAN.
THIS IS--YOUR SWORD--
--GRENADE BOY.

ALL BUNDLES DOWN.
所持品を下に置く!
WOMEN AND KIDS TO THE RIGHT.
女性と子供を右に!
TELL 'EM TO LINE UP FOR DE-LOUSING.
I DON'T KNOW THE WORD FOR "LICE."
TELL 'EM WE'RE GONNA SPRAY THE COOTIES OFF.
THAT'S A BIG HELP, SARGE.
JUST TELL 'EM SOMETHIN' IN JAP, OKAY?
JUST GONNA GET THE BUGS OFF THE KIDDIES, MAMA-SANS.
PUT YOUR GOODS ON THE PILE.
NO ONE IN CAMP WITH ANY PACKAGES.

IT'S *NOT* A WEAPON!

SWEET CHRIST.

28 JANUARY. USS MISSOURI.

FLAGSHIP OF THE THIRD FLEET. CODE DESIGNATE HORSESHOE.

DO YOU REALIZE WHAT YOU'RE ASKING ME TO DO?

MOVE TWO FLEETS. CARRIERS, BATTLEWAGONS AND GOD KNOWS HOW MANY TENDERS.

HAUL ANCHOR AND HEAD FOR OPEN SEA IN THE MIDDLE OF AN INVASION?

WE KNOW IT'S A LOT TO ASK, ADMIRAL.

ALL THIS FROM *ONE* DAMN RADIO TRANSMISSION? I *HATE* THIS SPY CRAP.

THIS IS A RELIABLE SOURCE. AND HIS INFORMATION CHECKS OUT, SIR.

THEY HAVE THIS WEAPON AND WILL DEPLOY IT.

WE THEORIZE THEY'LL USE IT AGAINST THE FLEET.

IT'S THE GREATEST CONCENTRATION OF PERSONNEL WITHIN THEIR RANGE.

WE START WITH AN UNACCOUNTED-FOR GERMAN SUB. THE U-217.
LAST SPOTTED OFF THE COAST OF IRELAND IN JULY OF LAST YEAR.
THAT'S TWO ***MONTHS*** AFTER THE NAZIS SURRENDERED.
CORRECT, SIR.

IN DECEMBER, A YOUNG GERMAN SEAMAN NAMED WILHELM MAHLMANN IS ADMITTED INTO A HOSPITAL IN NAGASAKI, WHERE HE DIES OF APPENDICITIS.
RECORDS SHOW HIS LAST DUTY WAS ON THE TWO-SEVENTEEN, DEPARTED BREMEN ON MAY 6TH.
JUST ***BEFORE*** VE DAY.
THAT SUB IS IN JAPAN.
WITH TWO CONFIRMED PASSENGERS.

KURT DEIBNER AND WALTER GERLACH. GERMAN PHYSICISTS WHO HAVEN'T BEEN FOUND. AND BELIEVE ME--G-2, MI-5, THE O.S.S. AND STALIN'S GOONS HAVE BEEN ***LOOKING.***
THIS PAIR ARE HOTTER THAN A THREE DAY PASS IN MANILA.

TWO EGGHEADS AND A KRAUT SUB.
AND I'M SUPPOSED TO SHOW MY TAIL AND MOVE ***TWO*** TASK FORCES?
IT'S ***MORE*** THAN THAT.

"GERLACH AND DIEBNER WERE THE PRINCIPLE PLAYERS IN DEVELOPING A SUPER-WEAPON FOR THE GERMANS.
"AND THEY CAME UP WITH A DOOZY.
"BUT THE REICH CAME TUMBLING DOWN BEFORE THEY CAME UP WITH A WAY OF DEPLOYING IT.
"IT WAS TOO HEAVY FOR ANY OF THEIR BOMBERS. TWO HEAVY FOR A ROCKET.
"WE BELIEVE WITH ALL CERTAINTY THAT THEY ARE IN NAGASAKI WITH THE COMPONENTS OF THAT WEAPON.
"AND THE MEANS TO DELIVER IT TO A TARGET.
"A MAN GAVE HIS LIFE TO BRING US THIS, ADMIRAL NIMITZ.
"NOW IT'S UP TO YOU TO MAKE SURE THAT SACRIFICE WASN'T MEANINGLESS."

29 JANUARY. SHIRAKAWA RIVER PLAIN.
ウォーター…
ウォーター…
WHAT'S HE WANT, JIMMY?
WATER. SAYS HE'S THIRSTY.
HUH.
BLAM!
THEY MADE IT THIS HARD, RIGHT? THEY MADE IT THEM OR US, RIGHT?
DON'T SWEAT IT, BARNES. THE WAY BACK TO THE STATES IS THIS WAY.
AN' THEY CAN GET OUTTA OUR WAY OR NOT.
ALL THE SAME T'ME.

13 FEBRUARY.
KUMAMOTO PREFECTURE.
MOTORS IN THE SKY.

WHAT IS IT?
YOUR LEADERS TURN YOUR COUNTRY TO RUINS. SAVE WHAT IS LEFT OF JAPAN. SEEK PEACE!

PAPER NOW.
NEXT WILL BE BOMBS.

LIES!

SURRENDER YOUR CHILDREN TO SLAVERY? YOUR WOMEN TO RAPE?
TO FIGHT IS THE ONLY PATH!

THE FUTURE IS WRITTEN IN YANKEE BLOOD!
WE FIGHT! WE FIGHT!

FEBRUARY 1946.
FUKUOKA PREFECTURE.
MILITARY ROAD DESIGNATED "MAPLE STREET" NEARING KURUME.
I SMELL APPLES.

THEY GOT APPLES IN JAPAN, JIMMY?
MY GRANDMA USED TO MAKE APPLE CUCUMBER SALAD.
SO I GUESS THEY DO.

AIR CORPS FLATTENED THIS TOWN, HUH?
ONLY THERE'S ALWAYS SOMEONE LEFT.
BETTER START SELLIN' YOUR WARES, JIMMY.

聴く!
誰も私を聞くことができますか?

TELL 'EM TO TAKE IT SLOW.
HARV... I DON'T THINK THEY CAN TAKE IT ANY OTHER WAY.

何かありますか?
SIMMONS! GET A MEDIC OVER HERE, PRONTO!
ALL I HAVE IS CHOCOLATE.
IT'LL HOLD 'EM TILL THE RELIEF COLUMN'S HERE.
IS GOOD? YOU KNOW-- OKAY?
OH KAY.
HOW MUCH MORE, BARNES? TILL THEY ALL BREAK LIKE THIS?
MAYBE THEY AIN'T BROKE. MAYBE THEY'RE ONLY HUNGRY.
SOON'S THEY GET A BELLYFUL THEY STICK A GRENADE UP YOUR ASS.
I SEE DEFEAT IN THEIR EYES.
THEN YOU SEE SOMETHING I DON'T, JIMMY.

4 FEBRUARY.
AIRFIELD ARIZONA AT NOEBEOKA.
YOUR TARGET IS NAGASAKI.
THIS IS MAXIMUM EFFORT. YOU'RE GOING TO LOCK THE PLACE UP TIGHT.
ROADS, BRIDGES, RAIL AND AIRSTRIPS. NOTHING IN AND NOTHING OUT.
EVERY BIRD AND EVERY CREW IN THE AIR AROUND THE CLOCK.
THEY TELL ME THE JAP HAS A SUPER WEAPON THERE.
I SAY WE HAVE OUR OWN SUPER WEAPON.
IT'S MADE OF AMERICAN BLOOD AND AMERICAN STEEL.
INTELLIGENCE ABOUT THE LOCATION OF THIS GADGET IS SKETCHY, AS USUAL.
SO WE'RE GOING TO RELY ON OUR USUAL STRATEGY, GENTLEMEN...

"...WE'LL BLAST THE PLACE TO *RUBBLE.*
"THEN WE'LL *BOMB* THE RUBBLE."
AIMING POINT DOGPATCH. BAY DOORS OPEN.
HOLD *ON* TO SOMETHING, GIRLS. WE'RE GONNA JOLT WHEN *THIS* BABY DROPS.
ROGER THAT.
TWO TONS OF "SO SOLLY" AWAY!

WAS IST?
音...
OUR LUCK REMAINS STRONG, ARNO.*
*TRANSLATED FROM GERMAN
IT APPEARS WE WILL NOT BE RETURNING TO OUR BERTH IN NAGASAKI.
WERE THE PENS TARGETED, OR WAS IT A MATTER OF CHANCE, CAPTAIN?
AND WHAT IS THE DIFFERENCE TO US, ARNO?
THE DIFFERENCE BETWEEN TEMPTING FATE AND BEING HUNTED, SIR.

THAT MINE MAKES A BASTARD OF MAINTAINING TRIM.
AS SOON AS WE REACH THE KUROSHIO CURRENT WE CAN RELEASE IT, THEN DIVE AND FIND A SAFE MOORING.
NOT A MOMENT TOO SOON, CAPTAIN.

RUNNING ON THE SURFACE. NO AIR COVER. ONLY OUR DECK GUN FOR PROTECTION.

ALWAYS GLOOMY SKIES AND ROUGH SEAS WITH YOU, ARNO.
AND YOU SEE CAUSE FOR GLEE?
I DO.

NO GERMAN NAVY. NO GERMANY. WE ARE THE LAST BOAT FOLLOWING THE LAST ORDER.
OUR WAR WILL SOON BE OVER.

AFTER TODAY, WE WILL BE... WITNESSES.

5 FEBRUARY.

KURUME RAIL JUNCTION.

DOES IT SNOW IN TEXAS, HARV?

UH-HUH.

USUALLY GONE THE NEXT DAY.

WE ONLY GOTTA **WIN** FIRST.

EYES FRONT!

MOVE SLOW-- SHOW YOUR HANDS!

SLOW!

CHECK 'EM FOR GRENADES, HARV.

JIMMY, TELL THESE BOYS WE AIN'T GONNA ***HURT*** 'EM.

EH?

WHERE'S HE GOIN'?
SAW A KID!

BABY SAN?

MUH NAME ISHI.
OH.

YOU SPEAK ENGLISH, ISHI? A LITTLE?
LOOK, I GOT FOOD.
DOZO. OISHI.

ISHI FREN'S.
AMEKO EADA SHEE.

SON OF A BITCH...

6

FEBRUARY.

THE USS SAN JACINTO.

TAKE IT, GRIFF.

THANKS, GEORGIE.

YOU LOOK LIKE **HELL.**

I'M FINE.

JUST WAITIN' FOR THE BALL TO GO UP.

THEY'RE FUELING US NOW, RIGHT?

RIO SQUADRON--RIO--ON DECK.
THAT'S US.
RIO SQUADRON--ON DECK FOR PRE-FLIGHT--

ORDERS ARE SIMPLE, BOYS.
TARGETS OF OPPORTUNITY.
TURN NORTH-NORTHEAST TO TARGET AREA BLUE NINETEEN.
ANY SHIPPING HEADING WEST PAST KABA-SHIMA IS GAME. IF IT'S JAP AND IT'S OUTBOUND-- SINK IT.
THAT SUIT YOU, GEORGIE?
G. BUSH
SUITS ME FINE, GRIFF.
THEN FORM UP ON ME AND KEEP YOUR EYES PEELED.

SAME DAY.
ARMY HIGHWAY I-4.

SOLDIER? WHAT'S YOUR UNIT?
THIRD ARMY, SIR. SIXTH OF THE SECOND.
DO YOU HAVE AN **ASSIGNMENT,** SON?
WE WERE WITH A TRANSLATOR. HE'S DEAD, SIR.

THEN YOU NEED TO **REJOIN** YOUR COMPANY.
LOOK, I DON'T...
I NEED TO GO HOME. SIR.

THE JAPS HAVE THEIR KIDS FIGHTING US, SIR.
I CAN'T KEEP ON WITH KILLIN' KIDS.

BECAUSE IT **HURTS** YOU TOO MUCH, SON?

'CAUSE IT **DON'T.**

TWELVE MILES SOUTH OF MEI-SHIMA ISLAND.
BANK LEFT, SWIFTY!
SOMETHING HOT, RED?
I'M ON THE HORN!
SOME KIND OF CRAFT MOVIN' WEST AT A CLIP.
NAVY OBSERVATION TO ANY FLIGHTS IN THE AREA.
RIO LEADER TO NAVY PLANE.
WE HAVE AN ENEMY CRAFT IN SIGHT--AREA BLUE TWENTY TWELVE.
IDENTIFY TARGET, NAVY?
GEE-- LOOKS LIKE A MACKEREL WITH A COCONUT IN ITS MOUTH.
RIO SIX TO RIO LEADER. WE'RE CLOSE TO HALFWAY ON FUEL.
ON OUR WAY.
THEN TURN BACK HOME, GEORGIE. I'LL CHECK THE BOGEY SOLO.

MAKING SIX KNOTS, SIR!
DAMNED IF ARNO ISN'T RIGHT--
THAT MINE IS AFFECTING OUR SPEED.
AT THIS RATE WE WON'T BE IN THE KUROSHIO UNTIL DARK.
A PLANE, KÄPTN!
SINGLE ENGINE AND TURNING!
DECK! ENEMY AIRCRAFT TO PORT!
GET THAT GUN TRAINED!
JA, KÄPTN!

RIO LEADER TO ALL SHIPS.
SIGHTED ENEMY SUBMARINE--MAP REF BLUE TWENTY ELEVEN.
ENGAGING SAME.
MARK POSITION--HEADING DUE WEST.
THERE'S A MODIFICATION TO THE SUB--SOME KIND OF GIZMO MOUNTED FORWARD.
GET THE GUN TRAINED STARBOARD, HANS!
HE'S COMING AROUND FOR ANOTHER PASS!

COM PAC RELAY TO RIO LEADER--CONFIRM THE SUB IS JAP.
IT AIN'T ONE OF OURS. OVER.
COULD IT BE GERMAN MAKE--CONFIRM.
I'LL BE DAMNED...
INSTEAD OF SAYONARA--
--MAKE THAT AUF WEIDERSEHEN.
HARD PORT!
ENGINES FULL!

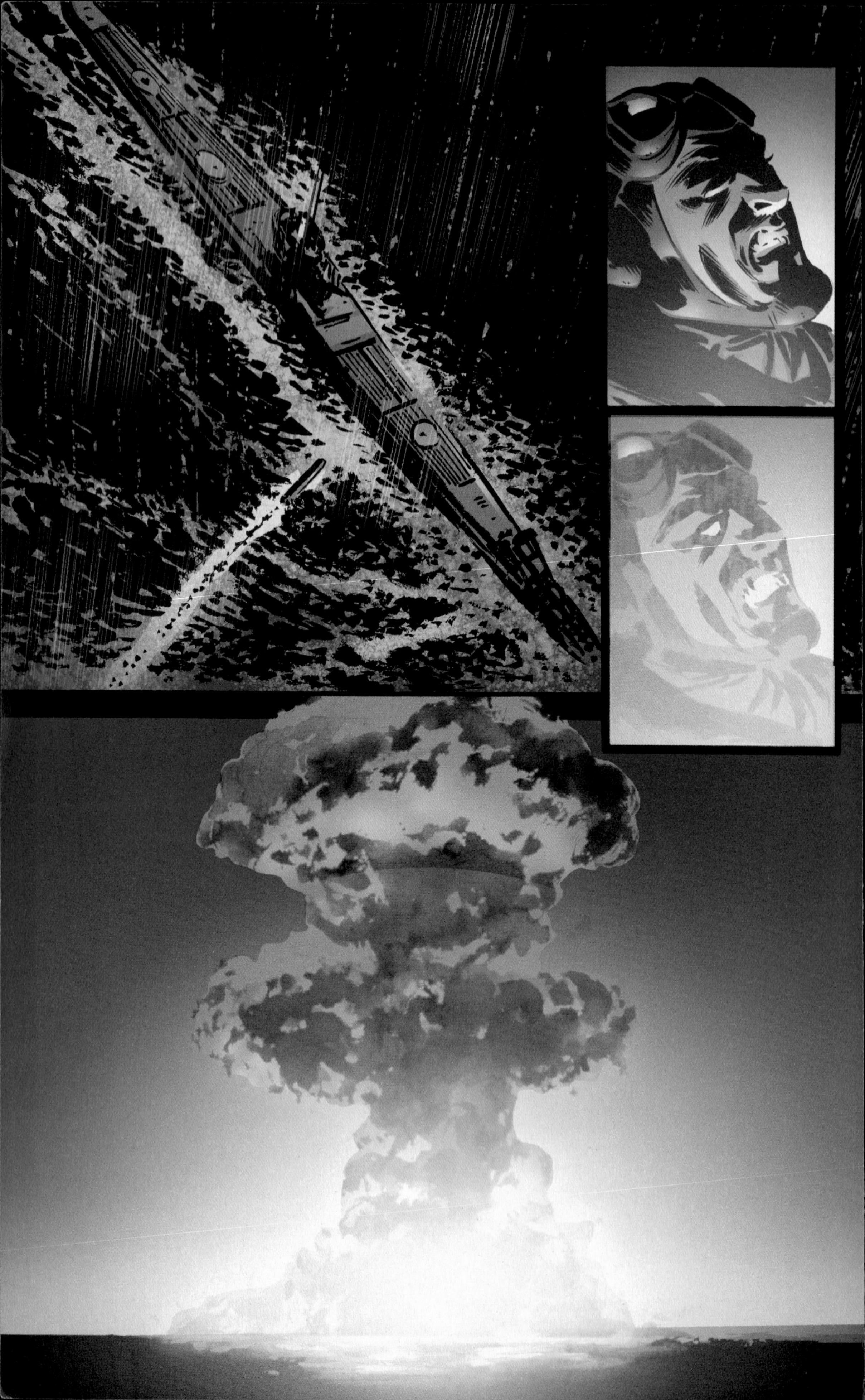

7 FEBRUARY.
THE PRESIDENTIAL RETREAT IN THE FLORIDA KEYS.
TOP SECRET FROM THE WAR DEPARTMENT, MR. PRESIDENT. IT'S BEEN DECODED AND MARKED RUSH-URGENT.
SOMETHING CERTAIN TO SOUR MY STOMACH, I IMAGINE.
WELL, SPIT IT OUT, SON.
HAND IT OVER AND STEP INSIDE, SAILOR. THERE'S COFFEE AND PIE STILL OUT.

THE JAP SUPER WEAPON. IT'S GENUINE, ED.
WHAT'S THE NATURE OF IT?
A BOMB. LIKE THE ONE OUR BRAIN BOYS TOUCHED OFF IN NEW MEXICO.

THREW UP A CLOUD TEN MILES HIGH. THEY HEARD IT IN MANILA.
DEAR GOD. WHAT IF THEY HAVE MORE OF THEM?

WE HAVE TWO OPTIONS, HARRY. KEEP FEEDING OUR BOYS INTO THE GRINDER OR NEGOTIATE A SURRENDER.
THERE'S A THIRD WAY. IT GALLS ME, BUT I'LL BE DAMNED IF I'LL SIT DOWN WITH THOSE YELLOW BASTARDS.

GET MOSCOW ON THE LINE.
SEE WHAT THEY'D WANT FOR THEIR HELP.

FEBRUARY 1946.
THE IMPERIAL RESIDENCE AT EDO.
WE HAVE HEARD FROM THE SWEDISH DELEGATION--
--THERE IS NO WORD FROM THE AMERICANS, HEAVENLY RULER.
THEY WILL SUBMIT. JAPAN IS ETERNAL, ADMIRAL.
I HAVE WRITTEN A POEM THIS MORNING.
TOUCHED BY SUMMER
THE FLOWER SLEEPS UNDER SNOW
TO WAIT SPRING'S RETURN
THAT IS ALL, HEAVENLY RULER?
THAT WILL BE ALL.
THE END OF
STORMING PARADISE